STAY STRONG

Sit in an I Am Enough Confidence

Norm Harshaw

Published by King & Justus Books, LLC
3030 NW Expressway, Suite 200 #568
Oklahoma City, OK 73112
www.KingandJustusBooks.com

First Edition
ISBN: 978-1-7376122-0-9

This book is dedicated to my loving wife Julia of 23 years who has put up with my many quirks and habits, she listens to my dreams and ambition and is always the rock that keeps me going.

To my kids Alec and Isabel who I have learned so much from as I watched and helped them walk through this world with all its difficulties and joy, laughter and tears.

My mother and father who helped me see life through many different lenses and have shown me what it was to be a father, husband and leader in my world.

Special thanks to Rick and Monique Justus, my King and Justus teammates, mentors and other family members who have helped me become who I am today.

TABLE OF CONTENTS

INTRODUCTION:

Thank you for picking up this book, you really don't know what you are about to get into but stick with me through to the end. I am quite raw and open with my own challenges with confidence in my personal life and in my 40+ years of business. We all have a grand challenge to solve in our lifetime. Most people suppress it and just get on with their lives, but really stop, pause, and give serious thought to the problem that your passionate about in the world and that you were meant to solve. Dig deep and find it, and don't just say world peace or world hunger—while these are excellent causes, we are unique, go big enough for it to be a challenge, but don't overwhelm yourself. Most people start in their neighborhoods, then branch out to communities, cities, and so on.

My grand challenge is what this book is about, and the title of this book; *Stay Strong and sit in an I AM ENOUGH confidence.* Self-confidence is one of the subject's personality researchers and mental health professionals most like to study. Thousands of journal articles have been devoted to it, along with dozens of books telling adults how to raise their own self-confidence or their children's (Harvard health-Harvard University). Why is confidence, or lack thereof, one of the most studied and written about subjects in the world? Because at one time or another; we all struggle, no one is immune. It doesn't matter your age, occupation, skin color, nationality, job type, or whether you are a professional athletes, actors, actresses, or politician, we all struggle the same. In fact, it seems the more in the public spotlight you are, the harder you must protect your confidence. This has been my struggle in my life over many, many years, something I have only begun to understand and take control of over the last 5 years. And only recently, with the writing of this book; I bring it to you. Because if you are honest with yourself—and be brutally honest, as this is the only way you will grow—you have struggled or still struggle with confidence. I am here to give you hope from a real-world view, learned in the trenches of life and business. This is street smarts, not book smarts. This is real, not manufactured stats in some lab or classroom where the researchers are living in a bubble—nothing wrong with academic papers but when is the last time you read one, or cared to?

This book is different, and I want to start out with something totally out of the ordinary, and I challenge you right off the bat to think and struggle with the concepts in this book. I will list the chapters out for you below, and I ask you think about the titles before reading any further. Take a picture on your phone of the titles below, write them down, whatever it takes for you to stop for a moment and think what they mean to you. We need to slow down as a society, we need to reflect more and think without the noise or distractions that consume us. There is also a word that goes with each chapter title that will help open doors to thought. Hint: these words are my purpose sentence; you will know what that means later in the book.

Here are the 9 ways to give you hope, to be honest with yourself, to stay strong in how to sit in an I AM ENOUGH confidence.

1. Gently – Don't be afraid to let others hear what they need to hear, gently.

2. Empower – Get quickly to the point that brings the relationship to life.

3. Leaders – Enter the conversation to build the relationship deep enough and in the right way.

4. To Stay – Dig down, find and pull the real you to the surface.

5. **Strong – Sit in an I AM ENOUGH confidence.**

6. In – Give yourself permission to be comfortable in the who of you.

7. Who – Embrace the power of who.

8. They are – Now, be and do you.

9. Become – Be and do more and more, consistently, forever.

I have been a parallel entrepreneur for almost 40 yrs. What is a parallel entrepreneur? Don't you mean serial entrepreneur? Well, funny you should ask, while I have owned companies at different times, I have always had several different streams of income coming in at the same time from my businesses; helping with a startup, helping a business exit, etc. This doesn't mean they always worked out, but I always have 3 or 4 legs on my stool. Never one business at a time, never just one income source at a time. I was never at the point of asking what do I do now—I jump, run, dive in and test the waters. There is time needed to put together the business plan or create the product, but most people never get started, you never feel ready, but if you have done the work, just go for it. We see this all the time, beta test after beta test, the product or service never making it to market. That's why a company dies every 3 minutes, it's just like having kids, you're never ready. There's never enough money saved, never enough preparation, never enough planning. If you haven't been there; when you bring your first kid home from the hospital, all your planning and preparation feels inadequate. But you get through it by sheer grit and determination and love.

Speaking of grit, I started selling Grit newspaper's in my small farming community when I was 10 years old, building my own small paper route. I would pre order the newspapers and buy them up front, learning early on what is called in the world of economics of "supply and demand," knowing that for each newspaper I didn't sell 25 cents would be lost, knowing that I could sell them for $1 and that my time was money. Building relationships was key, this wasn't about knocking on strangers' doors, these were friends and family that I had to give a good customer experience to because they knew my mom and dad. Reputation was my business card.

I knew all this long before I knew many of the current business buzzwords, I don't remember anyone teaching me these business principles. I'm sure my parents guided me in more ways than I can remember, and I'm thankful for their support all these years, even into adulthood. But I feel that much of what I knew at an early age came from the school of hard knocks and my natural ambition and intuition. I was street smart early on. I also remember during this time buying comic books for 5 cents at the local grocery store, knowing that I could sell them for more to my friends, but if not, they would be collector items someday. Did someone tell me about the time value of money or even what a collectable was? I don't know, but I knew how to make money, save money, and store money or products for a rainy day.

Talking about my natural abilities—we all have them, what I call pockets of Genius. Activities in business and life that you thoroughly enjoy doing, that you're good at, and people see you're good at them, and you get awards, compliments, personal joy, and satisfaction. We are all different and born with these abilities. Sure, you can learn new abilities, and you need to master your natural abilities, but they are there at birth. It's the same with your life purpose, your exact purpose in this life. This is not a vague sense of who you are, it's not what you do for a living, not the label other people put on you, but your exact purpose in one word and one sentence. That's what this book is about; my exact purpose—and here it is for you:

My purpose is to gently empower leaders to stay strong in who they are and become.

My purpose word is **Strong**.

Chapter 1

GENTLY – DON'T BE AFRAID TO LET OTHERS HEAR WHAT THEY NEED TO HEAR, GENTLY.

What is a real conversation? Is it small talk for 5 minutes at a party? Is it a networking event where you see how many cards you can gather only to spam them later with your product? Is it telling off your coworker or grumbling about your boss at the water cooler or on a zoom call? How many times have you needed to have a hard conversation about anything? It could be work related such as boss to employee, it could be parent to child, friend to friend, and the list goes on. Why is it so hard for us to have a hard conversation? Is it because we want to be liked and we are afraid of losing a friend or straining the relationship if we say the wrong words or the words come out in the wrong way? I'm here to say, don't be afraid to let others hear what they need to hear, gently. Make sure your motive in having the conversation and having your heart in the right place is top priority. It is not necessarily the words spoken, though of course words are important, what matters is if they come from a pure motive with love to soften the blow.

In this book, you will read about my love for horses and the psychology of being in tune with their body language, what you see and feel as you ride and work with horses. There are a million books on horses, how to ride horses, break horses, show horses, how to horse whisper, etc., and thankfully; this is not one of them. I am an amateur in all things horses, even though I rode for a span of 15 years consistently in my teen and young adult life. But many of the lessons I now employ in my personal life and business life were learned from my time with horses and the people who surrounded them. Still today, most of my lifelong friends were from this time in my life, and many of my fondest memories. I don't live in the past, but I learn from the past and keep the lessons close to me from the past so that I can live well in the present and cast vision for the future.

Here is one of my horse stories. Saddle up, as this story has everything to do with having a real conversation, gently.

In the old west as portrayed in the movies, a cowboy would throw a saddle on an unbroken horse (horse that has never been ridden before), another cowboy would twist the horse's ear so the first cowboy could get on the horse and get planted firmly in the saddle. The twisting of the ear was to distract the horse so the cowboy could get his feet in the stirrups and prepared for all hell to break lose once the horse realized something was on its back. The horse's survival instincts were about to kick in with the fury of a 1200-pound wild animal. I think you know, but don't realize, how powerful a horse is in real life, you will never win a war with a horse if they truly don't want to lose. The horses that won't give in to being tamed are sent to the rodeos as bucking horses; they are never tamed. In this scenario, the cowboy's whole goal is to break the horses will, he hurt the horse just to get on it, remember the twisting of the ear. There is not kindness here, nor gentleness, the mentality is; let's get the job done and move onto the next. The cowboy will win by using any means necessary. The cowboy will kick, gouge his spurs into the ribs, yank on the head with the reins, yell, curse, whatever it takes to be the winner, no matter the cost

How many of our conversations are like this old cowboy from the movies. Perhaps a person needs to hear what you have to say; this may be true, but how are you saying it? Are you preparing for a battle, are you biting and clawing with your words to make them hear what they need to hear, at least in your mind? Don't get me wrong, we all need to hear the words that are hard for us to hear, we all need to be coachable, but I don't want my will to be broken by your words. I will take coaching and correction from you in a loving and caring manner, gently, but if you come at me with spurs—I will not hear, I will not respect your right to tell me the words that can help me grow. You went about it the wrong way. You were not thinking about me, you were thinking this needs to get done so I can check it off my list. Where is the next unbroken horse that I need to impart my flawed wisdom on in the wrong way?

Some people thrive on breaking others, but most of us don't. I hope you don't, because soon you will be friendless in life. You may have power at work, but with no respect from anyone, hopefully your wife and kids still talk to you, and the list goes on.

Be the type of person who is not afraid to let others hear what they need to hear, but gently, with compassion, full of love, and a kind heart. To do this, you need to check your ego at the door, this is not about you, it should be about others. Again, if you are here to win the war, go back to your bunker, I don't want to hear from you, and I won't. I have too much respect for myself and self-love to let you into my mind and heart, I will get up from the table and walk away as soon as I see signs that you are not giving me words for my growth but for your own glory.

One of my past bosses (let's call him Rob) that I worked for in the summers as I was going to college had a very gentle but strong presence in my life. He was a master at having the hard conversations. When he would call you in his office, it was like "oh no, what did I do." However, many times, I knew what I'd done, but looked forward to the conversation with him, as I knew it would clear the air. Those in authority over us many times know far more about what we do than we realize. But they know what battle to pick so as not to tear down their employees. Similar to a parent, I am not going to call out every fault or mistake I see my child make, only the one that will build them up or will keep them from harming themselves.

It was this same philosophy with Rob, he only had the hard conversations that would help me grow and mature in business and life. Interestingly enough, he would not call me into his office, he would come and work beside me in the job, walk in my shoes, be more of a mentor for the time being than a boss. This helped ease the sting of the conversation and made his employees realize he ultimately cared for their wellbeing in life and business.

His conversations had the heart and compassion behind them where he could say anything he wanted to me, and I would accept it. I would desire to change and want the best for myself, and this is the outcome we should strive to deliver also. People will hear what you have to say when they know it comes from a strong place of conviction for their wellbeing with a compassionate heart for good. What are your motives as you talk with those in your life, business, or community? Be a light in the wilderness, and speak in love.

Another example comes from my daughter Isabel. In high school, she was elected to a position in an afterschool activity where she mentored and was in charge of 10 or so kids under her. She was, in essence, their boss, there was a hierarchy of command, she had someone to answer to also. These kids ranged from ages 15-18, both younger and older than her, a very delicate situation for a high school student to be among peers, yet she was there to help, guide, and mold. She had hard conversations, she had to call out extremes in personalities, from pettiness and jealousy, to laziness and hyperactivity. She did it with grace and poise. Sure, she struggled at times, myself and my wife counseled and shed tears with her as she grew into this position. But what made her successful was her genuine heart for those around her, they knew and trusted she had their best intentions in mind. And most of all; she was gentle and strong, while at the same time walking tall with the burden of leadership.

Have conversations that build up and edify those around you in both life and business.

Chapter 2

EMPOWER – GET QUICKLY TO THE POINT THAT BRINGS THE RELATIONSHIP TO LIFE.

Who here enjoys small talk all the time, every time? In the context of this chapter, I'm not talking about the start of a business meeting or boardroom meeting, I'm talking about one on one or small groups of people who get together to make business connections, do business, or sell a service to the individual or group.

I love having coffee with people, sitting across the table getting to know them, talking about business and life. Coffee makes sense, as I am from Seattle, where we have two coffee shops on every block and a drive through for those who need to drive and drink coffee.

Have you ever walked away from a meeting wondering what it was all about, what was the point? Either you talked only about business and it was an extremely cold feeling as you were just a dollar sign to the other person, or the small talk went on forever, and you never got to the point of the meeting. Not every meet and greet needs to have a business aspect to it, but if it is a tried and true business meeting, you must have a relationship. As the old saying goes; I only do business with those I know and trust. Time is a scare resource, we all only have 24 hours in a day, so while we need to build relationships for business, we can't take years to do it.

Another question for you: How can you get quickly to the point that brings the relationship to life? We are all different, there's no golden ticket here, but this is a tremendous question to struggle with. Have you ever meant someone who drew you into their circle, and the outside world seemed to melt away as you were the center of the conversation? You felt the other person was listening and actually hearing what you were saying. This doesn't happen very often, but it does happen. Go back and think about that person and what they did to make you feel an instant part of their world.

My wife Julia is one of these people, everyone loves her, wants to be around her, and most of the time she is the life of the party. She is a people gatherer, if you want to have a party or have a large group gathering, let her know how many, and she will get them there. She has unique and interesting gift that I believe is natural but also part of her training in her current line of work. She has a strong relationship with a large number of people, and if you sit down with her for the first time, within seconds you are best of friends. She brings the relationship to life. What's her secret sauce? Again, as in the last chapter, she genuinely wants to find the best in everyone and goes about it with love and compassion.

Since this is a business book also, what would it take for a sales person to have this power? It can't be about the sale; so many sales training are all about the close. Here are the 9 best closes to use, as we know a close must happen, but what if the potential client asked to be closed, what if they asked "how can I work with you" or "where do we go from here", "what is the next step?" In your mind, you're going hold on, stop, don't say that yet, I haven't used one of my genius closing techniques on you that I paid large amounts of money to learn at the Vegas conference with 5000 other sales professionals! I know, I've been there and done that.

Do it differently, get to the relationship quickly, with compassion, so that you're not wasting your time or their time. That being said, timing is everything, it may not be now, perhaps a year from now, but better to get to that point quickly and create a valuable relationship and bond than draw this out for another 5 years.

Empower yourself to be a person who brings the relationship to life, and quickly. But know you aren't meant to be in a relationship with everyone you meet or think you want to do business with. Not everyone is worth your time and energy; guard your relationships. Rick Justus, the founder of King and Justus, so amazingly coined the phrase, "Show me your friends, and I will show you your future." That hits close to home. We see this all the time in our kids, but what about in adult life in our personal and business relationships. Who do you need to release from your circle of friends and business associates or clients? Clients can many times cost us valuable time and resources when they are not aligned with your organization. Don't be afraid to let a client go, or fire them. One of my early bosses had this statement as he would let employees go from the firm when the core values didn't align "I want to give you the chance to be successful somewhere else." If they are really "special" clients, feel free to send them to your "favorite" competitor. If you know what I mean. This business strategy is not taught anywhere that I know of, so listen closely. Match up your trouble clients, those who suck your life blood, time, joy, and happiness, and give them as a referral to your favorite competitor who deserves them.

Speaking of competitors, this might be a good time to bring out one my favorite quotes from the book *Art of War* by Sun Tzu, "keep your friends close but your enemies closer." Know your direct competitors, those in your field of work, those who you like and don't like. As I mentioned; have the real conversation early on with a potential client to see if they are aligned with you and your purpose, mission, and vision of your company. If your whole inner spirit is telling you not to work with this client, then don't—listen to your gut. Don't let the dollar signs rule who signs up with you. An unaligned client will take up more time and energy and cost you far more money than they are worth. And what's more, do you really want a referral from this person? We are who we hang with, this client will know other just like them, whatever that looks like. So, if you want to have a happy, fulfilled day at work, fill it with people you like, who are aligned with you—both employees and clients. Get to the point in all aspects of your life where you can read, understand, and determine your relationships quickly with heart and dignity.

LEADERS – ENTER THE CONVERSATION TO BUILD THE RELATIONSHIP DEEP ENOUGH AND IN THE RIGHT WAY

I'm going to keep it simple here, when it comes to leading the conversation, leading the relationship, leading your company, leading your life, leading your family, and I could keep going, but I will stop to get us where we need to go—we are a leader in all we do, someone is always watching and learning from you. Even if you are not aware of it. In the least, you are leading yourself, and we don't live in a vacuum or bubble. Everything we do has repercussions on those around us. So, what is the best definition out there of a leader? Drum roll please… "A Leader it is one who leads."

So how do you lead in conversation? How does conversation build relationships deep enough and in the right way to get where you need to go? Again, I give you permission to not go deep with everyone you meet or want to know, as there are different level of relationships, as we all know. But for those clients who you really want to help, you have to get deep to really know their needs. Norm, are you telling me I need to go deep with my client to sell him/her one widget? No, not one, but 100 next week, a 1000 next month, a million next year. To sustain a long-term client or relationship, you have to get deep in relationship.

I had a phenomenal mentor in college who I will call Jeff. The first day of in person registration—yes, we didn't have electronic registration at this time in history— I had to flip through a 100-page catalog to find classes, write them down, turn into my class scheduler, then pray and hope they put me at the top of the pile for the 500-person class that 800 students were trying to get into. I stepped onto campus of this four-year institution of higher learning not knowing a soul. I didn't want to go where all my friends went to school, I wanted to get out of my comfort zone, be my own person, make a new life. I knew I needed to plug into campus clubs and activities to make friends and find social outlets. As is still the case today, the clubs line up around areas where students go for meals. There

22

are club fairs, outreaches, and prize give a ways—anything to make them stand out to the newly arriving students. All the club booths or tables were run by students but had adult advisors close by for questions or concerns students had. As I was talking to this one club student president, the advisor, Jeff, was listening. Jeff was nodding his head, not joining in the conversation, just there and aware. I started going to the meeting and making friends, and as I got to know Jeff, I was drawn to his genuine and real conversations. At the time, I was craving more than just fun and school, I was going through life struggles and life questions as every person does at this age. Jeff was able to build a relationship with me through conversation, and build trust, asking the right questions at the appropriate times to build it deep not just wide.

We all have the "wide" friends and clients, and I don't mean overweight, all the talk is superficial, no substance, after 5 or 10 minutes of chatting, you're done. It's really tough having coffee with the "wide" relationships, as you are out of conversation very quickly.

As I'm writing, I'm looking out my back yard at the 60+ year old white oak tree that towers over my backyard. It's majestic. My house is also backed up to a greenbelt with dozens of species of trees. Every winter during the storms, I see trees blown over or snapped in half. Many homes in my area have been hit by trees. A few years back, my wife and I were watching one of these storms from our window, watching the trees sway wildly, and in what seemed like slow motion, we watched a pine tree slowly descend and crash into our neighbors' house. It took out the kitchen and part of the living room. We ran over there to make sure they were okay. On another occasion, a house a few blocks away was completely cut in half by a tree during a storm. I have worried about my old oak tree in these storms and did some research. White Oaks have some of the deepest root systems of all trees in nature. Deep roots equal a solid base from which to continue to grow and flourish. This is what I am trying to get across to you in this chapter. Make deep, solid relationships with the right clients. Deep enough so that when that competitor comes knocking, which they will, you can have an honest conversation with them as to why they need to stick with you and your company. Price won't be an issue because they trust you, sure you have to remain competitive, but you don't need or want to be the lowest price.

Here is another tree story, then I will stop with the tree analogies. In my front yard, I had (I say had because I cut it down many year ago) a medium size tart cherry tree, it was only good for making cherry pies. I had several issues with this tree, but the biggest issue was that the root system was very shallow and running under my driveway. We all know what happens when roots grow under concrete; over time, they push up the concrete. Over many years, the roots were pushing up a whole section of my driveway, cracking it and making tripping hazards—thankfully no one has been hurt yet. The root system did not grow deep but "wide," harming my driveway, causing hazards, and developing dangerous situations. Taking this back to the relationships we have, they don't all have to go deep, there are certainly levels in our relationships with clients and friends, but the "wide" and shallow relationships should be met with caution. Don't spend time and energy on this type, and be very wary why that person is keeping you at arm's length or you are keeping them at arm's length. Trust your gut, if every fiber of your being is telling you to run away or be wary—listen.

For the right clients and friends enter the conversation to build the relationship deep enough and in the right way.

Chapter 4

STAY – DIG DOWN, FIND AND PULL THE REAL YOU TO THE SURFACE.

When was the last time you sat in a quiet place, or in your back yard at night with only the sound of nature around you, or took a drive to a park and walked with your thoughts? I am blessed to live in the Pacific Northwest, where we have lakes, forest, ocean, mountains all around where I can get away, even at lunch, to sit by a lake or watch the ferry boats traverse the Puget Sound. And there are times when I need a quick 5 minute break between meetings to refresh and sit in silence in my car in the parking lot. We are bombarded with distractions and noises. How often do you pause to take stock in yourself, to refresh, rejuvenate your mind and body? When was the last time you took time to reflect on the real you? What is your purpose, your exact purpose in one word and one sentence? Your purpose is not what you do for a living, not the volunteer work you do, not what you do for your family, not your religious beliefs, not what you do for recreation, not what you read—but the natural gifts and abilities that you were born with and that you have honed over the years. There is a lot of chatter out there in the business world about purpose, mostly sandwiched around mission and vision. Every organization needs a purpose, mission, and vision, but so does each person in an organization. Whether you are the CEO or the person answering phones at the front desk, you need to know your individual purpose which feeds into your pocket of Genius, which then feeds into the culture of the organization. If an organization can put their team members in their true pockets of genius, where they work most efficiently with peak performance and joy, the organization will be healthy and running at peak performance also. What do you truly enjoy, are passionate about doing, what brings you the most Joy in life and work? As I stated at the end of the introduction to this book, my exact purpose is to **gently empower leaders to stay strong in who they are and become.** This encompasses how I live in every area of my life. From my family, to my church, to volunteer work with nonprofits and causes I believe in. To how I talk with clients and friends, to how I wake up in the morning and go to bed at night. My purpose gives me laser focus to stay on the path that keeps me in my power, where I get the most joy and energy.

One of the hardest things I deal with daily is saying NO! I love to say yes, love to be involved, impart wisdom, give advice, be busy, love conversations over coffee over lunch or dinner, and the list goes on. I also perceive that it is much easier for most people to say yes than no. No is a negative (or is it), we feel it lets people down, robs us of Joy (or does it), pushes family, friends, and clients away, etc. If a salesman can get you to say yes 3 times, you are sold, you are a buyer of that product or service. However, you need to say no to the wrong things and yes to the right things, but what are the right and wrong things? You need a way to measure, a guide, a Sherpa to help you up the mountain so you don't get lost and die. Your guide is your exact purpose in one word or sentence. I put every business decision, every coffee I have, and every conversation I enter into in life and business against my purpose sentence. I know within minutes whether to say yes or no in most cases to the opportunities that come my way.

I have a big heart, and I am not afraid to say it, I want to help young people grow in knowledge and skill. I want the startup to succeed, I want the visionary to reach his dream, I want to invest in the right companies and markets, and the list goes on, but I can't do it all or help everyone. Because my purpose is who I am, I dug down, pulled out the real me to the surface, and I'm able to use purpose as my compass in all I do and say. My 20-year-old daughter Isabel and I are a lot alike, it drives my wife crazy, and that is the way we like it. Isabel has the most natural affinity with children that I or most people have ever seen. She walks into a room, and kids are drawn to her, they come up and want to play, talk, and be around her. She has babysat hundreds of times, been in church classrooms teaching, public school classrooms teaching, played with neighbor kids, it's always the same. When she leaves the babysitting job or classroom at the end of her time, the kids literally are blocking doorways, grabbing her legs, "Isabel don't leave, stay a little longer, please." Her babysitting kids cry most of the time at the end. We know adults who have this power as they enter a room, there is a presence that some people carry that we can see and are attracted to. It has nothing to do with status or money, being loud or outgoing. It can be charisma, but at some point, it is the real person, the heart and joy that stands out in a crowd, the confidence that they stand in knowing who they are, and that is enough.

Back to my daughter, because I am proud of her and love her very much, she is studying to be a teacher, oh and what a great teacher she will be. You know you can't fool a kid, not for long, they are like cats; they can sense if you don't like them or are not happy in the room with them. I am allergic to cats, so when I walk into a room and try to avoid them, next thing I know, they're in my lap. The kids sense and know that Izzy truly loves being in the room with them, wants to hear from them, sit, read, and play with them. She's not looking at the clock for the time when she can leave, her Joy and energy comes from the kids. As she's so young, most of this is natural talent—her wiring, who she is. She has natural instincts on how to talk and be around kids. She has a lot to learn, and that is what she's going to school to learn how to teach, but you can't teach love and compassion. At this point in her young life, I don't know her exact purpose word or sentence, but we will know it someday, and it will not surprise me or her but will bring her life; past, present and future, into perspective. After she graduates, she will go into teaching at the elementary level, but I could see her being a principle, or starting a business, or going to the moon, but one thing I guarantee—it will have something to do with kids and be centered around her purpose.

As I finish up this chapter, I want to tell you how I found my purpose. Sure, we need to be introspective, struggle with who we are, take the time to dig down, find and pull the real you to the surface, but I know you can't do it by yourself. I'm sure you have been in a forest or clump of trees and all you can see are the 15 or 20 trees right around you, the vast scope of the forest is not visible. This is an old adage. To find our purpose in one word and one sentence, we need help, someone to ask the right questions, ask who guided us through life's challenges, our greatest teacher's past, present and future. This is where I give a plug to Rick and Monique Justus, co-founders of King & Justus. They are brilliant and gifted in so many ways. They are the preeminent creators of abundant economies. This simply means that they have been co-creating abundant economies with children, citizens, CEOs, companies, cities, countries, and the cosmos for 35+ years now. You can look up their story at KingandJustus.com/rmbio. Helping leaders discover their exact purpose is a critical part of their Abundance Design process. In fact, they are the only 2 people that deliver exact purpose in the world. All to say, they helped me through this journey of exploration so I could find my exact purpose. I'm profoundly grateful to Rick and Monique for this gift.

Chapter 5

STRONG - SIT IN THE I AM ENOUGH CONFIDENCE.

We have all been there, at a party, social gathering, or networking event, and as I mentioned in the previous chapter, there is that person who lights up the room. Everyone knows who they are, even though they don't know everyone in the room. There is an aura that surrounds them, people are drawn in, they always have a crowd around vying for their attention. On the opposite spectrum, some people are popular because of their money, status in society, sports figures, movie or tv fame, or family name. Let me be careful here, they have their entourage, their "friends," but why are people around them; for who they are, or what they can get? I would encourage two things here, seek to always be a person of value, and seek friends and mentors who impart wisdom and value. These are the true and real people who light up this world, they bring Joy and Peace to those around them.

Sometimes these people have big personalities, are good public speakers, or boisterous at a party or networking event. They're able to shake hands and kiss babies. But, as mentioned before, what about the person who walks in the room, doesn't say a word, and you notice. He/she is smiling, full of joy and energy in their own way, there is an aura of confidence, an I am enough confidence. This allows them to sit at the table with any world or business leader or have coffee with the college kid who's looking for advice in getting his first real job. They treat and talk with everyone as the geniuses they are, not above or below others, they are comfortable in their own skin. Wow, how many of us can say that, how often we try to compare ourselves with others in our physical, mental, or emotional traits. We all do it, but we need to stop doing it. We need to be ourselves, because that is the only way to have the confidence to change the world. Being someone else won't do, you will never make the changes you need to make to leave this world a better place than you found it.

I previously bragged on my daughter, it is my right as a dad and author, now it is time to brag on my 17yr old son, nicknamed Al by his uncle. Sorry, son, I had to go there. His first love in sports is baseball and he's been playing it since he was in T-Ball. Having always been one of the bigger and stronger kids, he has excelled at all sports growing up. It's very interesting that he has chosen a rather docile and slow sport like baseball; however, he's a pitcher, an incredibly stressful and pressure filled position. I hope to write my next book on the lessons I have learned from his pitching career. It is an interesting position on the field, as most communication is nonverbal. The pitcher is the center of attention for players and spectators a large majority of the time. All the glory and defeat are heaped on the pitcher, every pitch could win or lose a game and there is no taking a play off or losing concentration. It is also one of the most injury riddled positions in all of baseball, not only from arm care, but pitchers are only 60 feet away from a ball coming off the bat in excess of 100+ miles per hour. In almost every game, the pitcher has a close call at the mound with a hit ball back at them. Many times they make fantastic plays, but just as often they are hit, and hit hard.

What's interesting about Al is that he has to be a strong imposing presence on the mound, both physically and mentally. He has the physical presence at 6'4" with the height of the mound being another 10-12" higher than the field. With his long stride and wingspan, by the time he releases the 80+ mile an hour fastball, the batter has only about 50 milliseconds to react on whether to swing or not. The ball is in the catchers' glove in 1.3 seconds after release. I say this to reiterate the physical presence a pitcher needs to possess to be successful, as this is the intimidation factor that they use. Of course, he must have the compliment of pitches to keep the batters off balance. Let's also get into the mental and non-verbal game, which is just as important.

The batters and opposing coaches will try and get in the pitcher's head with actions and words. A pitcher doesn't always have his best "stuff." He can be struggling that day with a curve ball or off-speed pitch that's getting hit hard, or he's walked the last two batters and the big homerun hitter is coming up. The bases are loaded with no outs, the pitcher is deflated, his head is down as he walks back to the mound. He's giving off many non-verbal cues, he has given up and, in most cases, he has failed at his job, his coach has lost confidence in him for now, and he may be pulled from the game. This scenario happens often, as there are very few complete games pitched in the game of baseball. But on the other hand, what about the pitcher who all of a sudden rises up and finishes the inning, gets out of the bases loaded jam, turns around the past failure to success, at least for the moment. I would call this the I AM ENOUGH confidence factor. The pitcher has a deep sense of knowing he can pitch in a way to win the war, sure he lost the last two battles with the batters, but he has won many wars before. He relaxes, takes a deep breath, and falls back in the confidence he has deep in his soul. I am enough, no more words needed from teammates or coaches, no need for encouragement from the crowd, his world goes silent as his laser focus and confidence takes over. As a fan, this turnaround has always amazed me; there is much to be learned in life and business from the sports world. You see this in football also, your team scores no points in the first half, few things are going right for them on either side of the ball. They go in at half time, and in the back of their minds, the fans are not wanting but expecting the same for the second half. Somehow, the offense scores a touchdown on the first drive, the defense makes a stop, and the game has flipped. Let's keep this in mind the next time you lose a big client, you get back reviews on your product, your day of sales are all "not at this time." Stick with it—your fortune will change, just as you are about to throw in the towel, you will score, keep the confidence up. By persistence, even the snail reached the Ark. An often quoted line from my favorite mentor to never give up.

Getting back to Al as a person, he is somewhat quiet, very level headed, not easily excitable or easily angered. He is not the rah, rah person in the dugout, hyping up the team. He encourages in a quiet, meaningful, and purposeful way, when needed and where needed. His personality translates well into pitching, and being on the mound, he must possess a calm, confident, and somewhat cocky presence. He has to be tone deaf to all outside noise, voices, and distractions. He gathers the nonverbal and pitching signals from his catcher, and the only voice he hears is from his coach on occasion. Between innings, he sits quietly on the bench, preparing his mind and body for the next battle, the next inning, again; no distractions, even from his own bench. Whether his team scores runs for him or not, whether he's ahead in the game or not, his focus is the same, no flinching, there's a steely determination with each pitch. As the starting pitcher, he sits in every second of the game with that I AM ENOUGH confidence that allows him to be successful. If for one moment he waivers in this confidence, the battle is lost, and worse; the war is lost for that game.

I love going fast whether on a horse, in a golf cart (story for another time) or in high performance cars. I have driven Formula 1 cars and a myriad of high end sport cars many times on Formula 1 tracks. In the U.S., Nascar is popular with the big oval track, and the drivers only turn to the left, but they go upward of 200 mph and use the traditional American muscle cars that we know and love so well. Nascar is a product of the U.S., it's why most Americans have more of an affinity for it, whereas Formula 1 automobile racing has its roots in the European Grand Prix championships of the 1920s and 1930s, though the foundation of the modern Formula One began in 1946 with the International Federation of Automobile's standardization of rules, which was followed by a World Championship of Drivers in 1950.

The cars are totally different, as are the tracks they race on. As I mentioned, Nascar is an oval track whose corners are left turning. The cars are built for the left turn banks, and drivers train for those left turn corners. On a formula 1 track or road course, there is usually one long straight away, but most of the track has left and right turns into flat corner turning. Most events occur in rural locations on purpose-built tracks, but several events take place on city streets. The Formula 1 cars are designed for extremely high cornering speeds achieved through the generation of large amounts of aerodynamic downforce, and the cars are highly dependent on electronics and aerodynamics, suspension, and tires. Depending on the length of the straightaway, the formula 1 can hit 150mph to 200mph, but it is only for a few seconds, as the corner is coming up fast. And as you can imagine, this being a road coarse track; it is all about the cornering and braking to gain the top lap times. Most of the passing of competitors is done around the corners, seldom on the straight away. All drivers can get close to the straight away top speed, but the true test of skill and nerve are going into, around, and out of corners.

In the last few months, I was in Vegas and drove this Corvette Z51 around the Speed Vegas track. To accomplish a fast lap time, I had to determine my minimum corner speed location (MCSL). If I hit my MCSL in the right spot turn after turn, I would nail my entry/exit speed balance and max my lap times. I had to slow down, to go fast. This took a high degree of trust in my tires, suspension, brakes, and my ability to shift and hit my location into and out of the corners. Before going full tilt on the track, I would spend a fair amount of time getting training and coaching on the track, the handling of the car, would watch other drivers, and take some test laps. By the time I was ready for the timed lap, I was confident in all aspects of the car and my ability to handle it and the track. I had to sit in the I AM ENOUGH confidence. Practice time was over, all lights were green, it is time. This chapter is all about this confidence that you have inside you, and if you have prepared properly, you need to go, full speed, full force. Use the brakes and shifter when needed, but step out in faith and GO.

Similarly, Business is not all 200MPH straightaways, there are corners, there are other competitors in front and behind you, jockeying for position, looking to win this race with a client. Don't let the race be all tactical you need to slow down or speed up; practice strategy, not just tactics. 89% of the people out there only practice tactics, no vision, they never slow down to look at the track now or what it might look like a year from now. What is your 20-year plan for your purpose, mission, and vision? What is your quarterly plan for sales? Driving fast and competing has everything to do with life and business, and hopefully this illustration has helped.

Are you strong in this way? In the I AM ENOUGH confidence as you walk through life, as you transact daily business? You have it in you already, the confidence. You might need to study and do some research for your next client to talk intelligently, but your confidence is already there, your wisdom will come forth if you let it. You can sit at the table with any one you choose, you can carry any conversation you need to have, you can impart your knowledge when and where it is needed, just step into it. We are all afraid at times that we will let ourselves, our family, co-workers, or bosses down, we might fail and lose a battle. But if you get up, dig deep, do the studies, research, and practice what you need to do with confidence, you will win the War. Win the mental war in your own mind, fight the negative inner congress of voices, and do your best—do what needs to be done to be successful in life and business. Use this daily affirmation or whenever you feel the negative voices start taking over:

"I am enough, and I sit in my confidence."

Chapter 6

IN - GIVE YOURSELF PERMISSION TO BE COMFORTABLE IN THE WHO OF YOU.

What does it mean to be comfortable in your own skin, to accept yourself as you are. Of course, you always need to be growing, living with more joy each day, helping those around you, and so on. But are you accepting the who of you? It's not up to me to define this for you, but I would challenge you to sit with the title of this chapter. Write, journal, talk about it with others, talk to yourself, really ponder what this might mean to you. Kids are great examples in this area; they don't worry, they just do and are themselves. Sure, they make plenty of mistakes, but they embrace who they are, they don't think about it, they are themselves for better or worse. Hopefully, we have more maturity to handle situations better than children, but we have lost the ability to do and be who we were created and born to be. We worry too much what others think of us, don't let the judgment of others change you. Be you.

One of my favorite clients who we advise with King and Justus is quite comfortable pushing the boundaries, being themselves in the public arena and with clients. They are a breath of fresh air in this politically correct charged world. They are who they are and will produce their products, if you like them, great, buy them, if not, they accept your criticism, but it won't change their products. They are comfortable in their own skin. In fact, one of the words in their mission statement is Weird!!! Isn't that interesting and refreshing? They call themselves weird and are excited about it, this gives them energy.

One of my mentors and good friends is a cowboy through and through, he is a brilliant businessman and lights up a room when he walks into a crowd. He is a big presence with his physical stature and booming voice, but you can see his heart, joy, and love for people. That is what really shines through. He legitimately will listen and have a conversation with anyone, he sits on boards in all areas and imparts wisdom. As I mentioned above, he is a cowboy, a real cowboy, he has horses and still rides even though he's getting older. Now and then, he does cattle drive or two a year. The kicker here is that he lived in the Seattle WA region for 55 years dressed in full cowboy regalia.

He would travel all over the state, downtown Seattle, meeting in high rise building, corporate headquarters etc. dressed to the nines in cowboy boots, jeans, belt buckle, and Stetson hat. He was who he was meant to be. He understood the who of you, the who of himself. He always took his hat off when entering a building out of respect, as that is what a cowboy with manners does.

People noticed how he dressed, it was different than most, really different depending on the venue, but he brought light and life to a room. People were drawn to him, they wanted to meet him, shake his hand, talk for a little bit and stay in touch over the years. I have described my friend in many words here, but the confidence he exhibits in himself, in who he is, in what he could leave you with, is Joy. It is this man's gift to the world. He is confident in his wisdom, in his surrounding, in his own skin, in his speech, in his preparedness for a meeting, and the list continues. Be and become fully invested in yourself, whatever this may look like for you.

Another example of a hero of mine who was comfortable in who they were was my grandmother Alice. She passed away many years ago, but many of my childhood memories are from the business her and my grandfather ran together for 20+ years. It was a rustic style resort on a fishing lake in the middle of Washington state. The fishing season on this lake is only open for 4 months a year in the spring. Needless to say, this was haymaking season for my grandparents, it was 7 days a week 7am to 9pm for those 4 months. Sure, they hired some extra help, and my mom and dad would help on the weekends, and my sister and I would get into plenty of trouble taking care of ourselves. We definitely had guardian angels looking out for us, because a few of our adventures we should not have survived. I won't go into the details here, that is for another book. Back to my grandmother, she is my hero because of the constant health issues she battled her whole life with diabetes. Before she passed away, she was the oldest living type 1 juvenile diabetic in the U.S. as she lived to be 76 years old. The story goes that soon after insulin was discovered for type 1 diabetes, she was diagnosed. I don't know the exact length of time here, but close enough that she told us grandkids the story. Because of her long-standing battle as a juvenile diabetic, the health problems continued to mount over the years, from battling degenerating eyesight, circulation problems with hands and feet, to hardened arteries in her heart. But she never complained, never used it as an excuse to not be the best version of who she was to family, friends, and customers. She was beloved by her customers, by the fishermen who came year after year and the local townspeople who she interreacted with on a daily basis. Even though she often times did not feel well or was having a bad day, you never knew it, her joy and love of people was bigger than her problems. I don't know where she got this strength to work as hard as she did, but she was secure in who she was. She had the confidence in her physical and mental health to overcome the obstacles of being a juvenile diabetic. She had the confidence to run a business, work hard, and overcome the daily adversities that came her way. Sure, she was not perfect, no one is, but I learned a lot by watching her run her business and do life at the same time. My grandmother's name was Alice, to keep her memory alive and well, we gave this as my daughter's middle name.

Chapter 7

WHO - EMBRACE THE POWER OF WHO.

I love definitions of words, and I really love digging into their meaning. I feel this is being lost in today's fast paced, multitasking society. Here is the definition of Embrace, it is an act of accepting or supporting something willingly or enthusiastically. Put this definition into context of everything we have talked about in previous chapters. Having the real conversation, building relationships in the right way with those that you want and need to, dig down and discover the real you and bring it to the surface, sit in I AM ENOUGH confidence, and be comfortable in the who of you. So here it is, after all this work, have you arrived? Not yet, there are a few more steps to being the person and leader you need to be in life and business. I mentioned the definition of embrace above, and this is where I am now going to come in strong. You have to accept who you are and have always been, as you just brought it to the surface. You have just stepped into your power, regardless of what others think or feel about you. This is who you are, embrace it, accept and fully support yourself, willingly and enthusiastically. Once you find your purpose, your exact purpose word, it will be a quick and solid reminder, consistently, of who you are. You have already grabbed what you found inside of you and pulled it to the surface, now live it with conviction, use it to help yourself and others. For definition here, the power of Who is you to the full extent of your power and who you are really; the who of you.

Here is a story of someone close to me, who I loved very much, and in the last couple of years has embraced her power of who she is—my sister. We get along well now that we are older, but like all brothers and sisters, we argued and bickered growing up. However, being 4 years younger than me, it didn't get really bad. I graduated and left home for college at 18, she was married by 21 and moved to the other side of the country, so we have been more like long distance friends with a family bond over the last many years, if that makes sense. So, in essence, for the last 20 years, we have talked on the phone, taken some family vacations together, but I feel like I didn't really know her anymore. However, over the past couple years, life has thrown her some curve balls, and I have seen a tremendous transformation, similar to what is described in this book. The adversity has forced her to be more independent, she has discovered and had to dig deep to find her real self. I talk about having real conversations with other people; well, I know she has been forced to have real conversations with herself. I know for a fact that she has won the war and embraces who she is now. Actually, she was this person all along, it was just buried so deep that it took pain to bring it to the surface. She now has a wonderful group of ladies who empower and motivate each other to be the best they can be in life and business; she has a wonderful career working with and changing the lives of kids every day, and she is able to be a mentor to younger women. She has accepted the challenge that has refined her with fire, and she has embraced the power of who she is with conviction and determination.

Just as my sister did, once you have done this for yourself, you will need to lead others. Be a leader. Again, we are all leaders, we all lead in different ways, in different situations in life and business. You don't have to be the CEO of a large company to lead, and remember; people are watching. Here is a challenge to the CEO, COO owner of the company, however big or small, mid-level managers, and the list goes on. Do the people under you, those who report to you or your mangers see themselves as leaders? Just because you have a title doesn't make you a leader and not having a flashy title doesn't let you off the hook of being leader. In the movie Ford vs Ferrari, the Ford motor company was losing market shares to Chevy at a high rate, they were struggling for ideas on how to stay on top. Henry Ford II walked out to the manufacturing floor, shut it completely down, and made a short speech to all assembly line workers that went something like this, "I want every one of you, as you are walking home tonight, to ruminate on your job and the Ford motor company, and come back tomorrow morning with a new idea, if you don't have any ideas, don't bother coming back to work." This is my interpretation, just because your job is to put lug nuts on a wheel does not give you the right to not think, bring new ideas or lead in this company. I don't care if you have been with a company 1 day or 40 years, the moment you get complacent and comfortable is the moment you cease to be valuable. Company owners and CEO's, help each of your employees to be a leader, give them permission and show them how. Employees, if you really love your company and who you work for, step up and be a leader, you don't need a title, just bring energy, focus, and joy to your work. Look for ways to make the company better, your departments better, your job better. If you have embraced the power of who, then make a difference in your world around you.

I will again go back to my daughter Isabel as an example of her embracing the power of who by helping others, both her peers, those younger, and those adults in charge. Isabel spent 4 years in high school in a high-performance showband, this was not your average parade marching band. Performed on a football field, this was precision playing, formations, performances, and drills done by the band on a show circuit. It really is something to behold that 14 to18-year-olds get to a level of drill precision, execution, and discipline only seen by the elite college bands that give performs in this way also. Her school was one of the top high schools in the Northwest of the United States, so they were very good and very serious. I estimate the band members put in 250 hours of work in before their first show. Isabel was always a leader among her peers, even without the title. The physical and mental strain of training and drilling would cause kids to quit or want to quit. They would sprain ankles, knees, get heat exhaustion, or just struggle to keep up, she was always there as a positive reinforcement, a real guardian of the mood, like all good leaders should be. But her Junior and Senior year, she took on official leadership roles within her section and band as a whole. Since she had been leading all along, sure she had a title now, but what she did for those around her didn't change. She more fully embraced who she knew herself to be, helped guide and lead her peers, and, more importantly, was able to emotionally help the younger band members. It was especially hard on the freshman, as they didn't know what to expect, didn't know many other kids, and were genuinely very nervous about the whole experience. She took it upon herself to go above and beyond what was initially required to help where needed; it could be in other sections of the band that needed extra help or the student leader who was not up to the task. It could be serving in a way that she felt would help the freshman adjust or stepping up and encouraging, bringing laughter and brevity to a tough situation. She would help them embrace the situation and see themselves fighting a battle, encourage them to get through it and win. The lesson learned from Isabel to us is that you need to make sure you are in the best place you can be and then come alongside others in the ways mentioned in this book. Only by working on yourself first can you be in your full power of who.

Chapter 8

THEY ARE - NOW BE AND DO YOU.

We are getting down to it, congratulations on coming along with me in the journey of this book, and I do not say this lightly. This has been my journey; these chapters are born out of my purpose word and sentence. I swear, I have had more introspection over the last year and a half since receiving my purpose than my whole 40+ years to this point. Not that I didn't know who I was, I was doing, succeeding, living, and loving, but it was out of instinct coming from my natural abilities. Nothing wrong with this, but it is much more messy way to live; my road had many twists and turns, sometimes I went in the ditch. There were times I stayed in the ditch, not knowing whether to go north, south, east, or west. My road map was blurry, I still had a sense of where I was going and knew I would get there someday. But now, with all I have shared with you, my road is paved, my map is clearly marked with my purpose in mind, and each exit is judged through the lens of purpose. If I get off on the wrong exit, a project doesn't work out, or an investment goes sideways, I can find my road and get back on quickly. It is often the time spent on a wrong turn or exit that costs us precious resources. People have lost years or a decade or two figuring out where they went wrong, searching for the right road or next project. Most people are never sure if they are on the right path or road, but at least they are moving forward, making some money, investing for retirement. That is their main goal; to retire. Then they will do their dreams of travel, live on a lake, see the world. Nothing wrong with retirement, but don't use the planning of it as an escape from reality. If you are only working to retire, you will be sorely disappointed, as this road too has potholes and ditches, and all of a sudden, they lost their way again. Don't wait to do all that is in your heart, do what you love to do now. In the final page of this book is a great study on millionaires and who they are. Only by being yourself, finding yourself and your purpose, will you go where you need to go in this life. People are waiting for you to show up and solve your grand challenge—what you are meant to solve here and now

Let's put this chapter title into the first-person form— Now I can be and do me. The struggle is real and continues and will continue as you grow and become more and more. The more I think about and struggle with this, the more clarity comes.

One time in a business meeting someone asked a very good question, I had an idea of the answer as there is usually more than one solution to a problem. For some reason, this time, I said, "great question, I have an idea but I want you to ponder your question, struggle to find a solution." It was not at a critical juncture for the business, so there was time. I had never said that before or since, and I don't advise doing it often, but that time, it was right. I also never give out wisdom or advice that I don't do myself, and because I struggle and want to struggle with questions and answers, this worked. Now be and do you. No more excuses. Sometimes it gets messy, that's okay. It will never be perfect, but most of the time others can't tell. We are too hard on ourselves to be perfect, have perfect lives, perfect hair, perfect job, perfect family, and the list go on. However, now is the time, now is your time—let's go!

In an earlier chapter, I mentioned my wife, I call her Jewels, as she is very precious to myself, our kids, family, and friends. I also mentioned that she is a gatherer of people because they know she have a real love and care for them. We have been married 23 year, we meant 3 years before that, so for 26 years, I have known her, and the old adage, "what you see is what you get" is so true with her. She is the epitome of Now, be and do you. I wonder even in her teen years if she ever doubted or tried to "find herself," there is so much confidence and comfort in the way she lives life, it blows my mind. Another one of her gifts is reading a person's emotions. She can be talking to someone and afterward says "by the look in their eyes, I can see how they are feeling, I sense what is really going on behind the scenes." I don't understand, but she will come away after just meeting them and say they are sad or angry or happy or peaceful. Some of this has been the training and experience for her line of work, but a large percentage is natural ability, who she is. You have to have a real love, joy, and heart for another person to care enough to see them. I have to be careful here, she jumps 100% into all activities, with the innocence of a child not caring what you think, just doing what needs to be done, and in most cases for other people. That is why she is such a good gatherer of people. She will do what is needed to make you successful, make you look good and ensure you win. Notice what I just mentioned—she is thinking of others always, however; not putting herself down in the process. Many times, someone will elevate others or help them win only for self-gratification. Maybe they get a raise, job promotion, or jump in social status on the coat tails of this other person. If I help get Joe the promotion, it will look like I am a team player and I care about his welfare, so this elevates myself for the next promotion. I can think of worse reasons to "help," but the motive is not right, and people will see through the façade. People will know you are not genuine when you compliment, and will question your motives. You will not grow or have real joy, as it is not who you are authentically. You have already done the work, or should do the work to make yourself and this world a better place, so don't spoil it. Run, now, into the authentic you, the real you, and don't be afraid to let people see you in your power. Be the genius you already are, there is no one else who can be you, we are all individuals.

You don't need this, but I give you permission, right now, be and do you.

Chapter 9

AND BECOME - BE AND DO MORE AND MORE, CONSISTENTLY, FOREVER.

In the game of life, there is no neutral. Physically, you are getting stronger or weaker, mentally you are learning to stay sharp, or brain cells are dying, causing memory fades. The same in your professional life; learning new and becoming sharper in your knowledge or slowly falling behind the competition. Finding win-win solutions or losing in battles, seeking abundant economies for yourself and those around you or cowering in the corner, living in scarcity with an ever-increasing fear and darkness surrounding you. This last sentence may sound harsh, but we BECOME or we don't. For me, become is a present and future process of growth. I told you I like definitions. Become; a verb, "to come or grow to be." As a side note, becoming is an adjective or noun, why the distinction here, you are wondering? Because I feel that this word, become, which is the last word in my purpose statement, is the 2nd most important word behind my purpose word 'Strong.' Let's look at my purpose again; 'to empower leaders to stay *strong* in who they are and become.' BECOME, a verb and action word, a never-ending struggle to do more, be more, have more, live more abundantly each day in life and business. You never arrive fully, and that is okay, the moment we think we have arrived is the moment we stop growing. The moment we settle for something less than who we are and are meant to become is the moment we look behind and not forward to the future.

At my purpose day, I questioned the wisdom of this word with Rick and Monique Justus. At the time, I thought it should be becoming, it just sounded better, I guess. Rick stuck to this original word, Become, he knew that was it, didn't know for sure why, that was for me to figure out. So glad he didn't cave in to me at the time, or this book would not have been written. You see, this book is part of my journey, an action for my continued growth to become all that I can be and do. For me, my family, and the world around me. In this process to become, I have to be consistent every minute of every day to see, grow, and learn from the people around me, learn from the circumstances I am put into, find the hidden lessons, and seek the nonverbal cues. I have to be available, always vigilant, and voice the words of wisdom that come to mind.

One of my clients said something profound the other day that made a great impact on me. He said that after being with us for a few months in our coaching and training program, and I paraphrase here, "as I was driving to work today, I actually noticed the leaves on the trees for the first time, the world around me slowed down as I noticed my environment more and more." I realized that is where I like to be all the time, not just once in a while, but I have to be consistent at this. It is like being in the eye of a storm, calm and peace while chaos is going on all around you. You hear and see the storm, but you choose to not let it sweep you up in its mess or distract you from your mission; you must remain in control. Remain in control of your mind, body, and spirit, and remember one of a leader's jobs is guardian of the mood. This consistency must be forever, until you take your last breath on this earth.

Forever is a very long time, yup, but that is your calling. Again, the title of this chapter: <u>And, be and do more and more, consistently, forever</u>. And never stop doing good, and never stop living your best life, and never stop living in joy, and never stop living in an abundance mindset to be the best version of you. I could write another book if I keep going, maybe I will, but not here. You really didn't think I could write a book about all I have learned from the most important people in my life and not get to my mom and dad. The true heroes in my life, who taught me how to work hard, respect, and be courteous to all peoples, how to handle adversity and live with conviction. My parents have been consistent with those in their lives as long as I can remember and before I was born. They unselfishly gave their time, energy, and love to family and all who would receive. My mother has not had an easy life, and she has every right to be inward focused and selfish. Her mother died when she was 17, her dad wasn't around much, she lived with relatives until she graduated high school, put herself through college to become a nurse with little to no help. She and my father met and married in college, they had me a year later, then dad got drafted to Vietnam. He wasn't supposed to get drafted, as he was married, in college, and had a kid, but his number came up, and he went. Even with money coming in from the military, she struggled to make ends meet, not able to work with a baby. She tells me stories of her going hungry and using powered milk mixed with water to feed me, her young son. Financially, things got much better as dad was able to leave the military, graduate from college, and get into the work force. Mom was always there for the family; she would go to work when needed for extra income and work to help put my sister and I through school. Again, a story of consistency to her family and friends, she never complained just did what needed to be done. Even now at age 73, my parents are finally empty nesters. Wait—if my younger and only sibling graduated high school in 1989, how are they finally empty nesters in 2019? In the last 30 years, they have helped raise, on two separate occasions, two boys. One was 6 years old whose grandmother passed away, and one 8 years old whose dad had passed away and the mother was no longer around. By taking them into their home from the young ages through age 18, my parents kept them out of the foster care system, helped them graduate high school, and gave them a loving and caring home. Currently, one is married with kids and has a successful career in the IT world, the other just left for college and is majoring in Business/accounting. I can almost guarantee that if it weren't for my parents taking these young boys into their home and raising them, they would not be in the place of success they are now. My parents did more and more consistently to bring joy to this world.

My father did well in the world of business, always respectful and respected. He went through some tough times, as we all do, but he always wanted to do what was best for his family and the company he worked for. When he retired at age 65, my parents were living in a small farming community in Eastern Washington state. The tiny church they attended suddenly lost the pastor. It can be rather hard to find a pastor willing to come to a small town in the middle of wheat fields, especially at the pay scale this small church could afford. So, guess what, my dad, only a few days after retiring, stepped up to be the pastor and started another career which would last until age 75. He just retired again a couple months back. We will see if retirement sticks this time, but I doubt it. The lesson here is always be and do more, you are never too old or too young, and be and do forever. Until my dad passes away, he will not slow down or quit, he will see hurting people in the world and help, see problems that need solved and solve them, see communities or cities that need leadership and step up. This is my legacy, I have to live up to this, I have no choice, and that is why I have written this book. I challenge you to struggle with the here and now, the future of your legacy for future generations. Lead with joy and an abundance mindset to change those around you, change the business environment you work in, be different, do different, the haters will hate but secretly admire your vision and determination, forever.

No Conclusion Here, I Don't Believe in Them, as This Is a Never Ending Struggle to Become:

Sit in and continue to become the best version of you. Fully take it in, fully embody your exact identity, stay, remain, be stronger in the who of you, you got this, and you were born for this moment. You notice it is sit, not stand up and shout it from the roof tops, although, someday you will have this opportunity. But sit and be intimate in your confidence, you want more growth, more transformation, more becoming, and I implore you to go further. Continue to transform in the gift of who you already are, and become. Stay strong forever, consistently, not once in a while, but every minute of every day.

I started this book out with a story about horses, and I will end it that way also. As I was going through college, my summer job for 4 summers was working at horse camps, breaking horses, teaching kids how to ride, taking guests out on trail rides, mucking stalls, and many other more disgusting things I will not mention here. My favorite activity was teaching kids and adults how to ride a horse, not an easy thing to teach, as you are dealing with a small human on the back of a big animal, many things can go wrong. Mostly what I was teaching at the lower levels was building the confidence of the rider to control the horse under them. All a rider has to control their horse are two pieces of leather (reins) connected to a small piece of metal (bit) in the horses' mouth. Yes, you, the 60 pound 11-year-old girl, can control this 1200-pound horse. Confidence. I wanted to bring my teaching up in this context, as I feel the most effective teaching times were done while instructing from the back of a horse. I would **sit** horseback in the riding arena with them while they were riding. I could have easily just stood in the middle of the arena (which I did do also) but sitting on a horse while they were also on a horse, built comradery with them and gave them the confidence that I knew how to do what I was teaching. What is very interesting, in the higher levels of English riding such as *dressage,* is that the hands (on the reins) do very little to control the horse, they are called "having quiet hands." The shifting of your body weight, the way you sit in the saddle (your seat) and your legs are used almost exclusively in the training process and the show ring. It is often said that the rider with the great seat is a greater rider. Another analogy to sit in confidence, as is written throughout this book

Have you ever been in a classroom setting where the teacher sat and taught? I had an older professor in college who used to sit in our large lecture hall and teach. As strange as it sounds, I felt closer to him because he sat and taught, even though there were hundreds of us in the class. When you sit, you become closer to those you are teaching or lecturing, when in a meeting, you all sit together, whoever is leading the meeting usually sits also. To have the real conversation, you need to be eye to eye, be able to connect person to person. If you are in a situation where you must have the authority, you will stand while everyone else is sitting. You get the point here, I hope.

Sit in, reflect, and gain the confidence to be who you were called to be.

FINAL THOUGHT

I pulled this excerpt out of one of the books written by Rick Justus that deals with our negative or positive thought life around abundance. "Dr. Martin Seligman, in his book, *Learned Optimism* didn't just find that negative people get sick more often, got divorced more frequently, and raised kids who get in more trouble. He found that negative people make less money. He conducted a long-term study of 1500 people. In group A, 83% of the people took their particular jobs because they believed they could make lots of money. Interestedly, in Group B, just 17% took their jobs because they loved their jobs. Twenty year later, both groups produced 101 millionaires. Only one millionaire came from group A. 100 of them came from group B. what is even more telling; more than 70% of these millionaires never went to college. Attitude, more than aptitude, determine altitude." Confidence brings real happiness, joy, real conversations, and the ability to be, do, and have all you were put on this earth to accomplish.

ABOUT THE AUTHOR

Norm is the CEO of King & Justus Abundance Day. Abundance Day is the culmination of a 34+ year global study where you will be introduced to four powerful processes: How to Love, How to Live, How to Give, and How to Enjoy. Their practical wisdom will equip and empower you to truly master all 12 Practices of Life so you can achieve abundance 20 years faster. You can visit King & Justus Abundance Day at www. KingandJustusad.com.

Prior to King & Justus, Norm spent more than 27 years gaining deep experience and expertise as an entrepreneur, founder, CEO, and Managing Partner across industry verticals, including finance, insurance, lending, and many more. Past experiences include buying and selling businesses, international finance to small countries, and corporate fundraising. With a heart for economic abundance, Norm always the change agent, learned early on to never quit.

Drawing on his years of client and international experience. When Norm is not involved in the flow of money at every level, he may be found enjoying Julia, his beautiful bride for 23 years, his two children, Isabel and Alec, or a good book. He is a global explorer, and will one day soon find himself on a Rhine River cruise. Addicted to speed, he loves to ski, ride horses, race cars, and time travel.

CPSIA information can be obtained
at www.ICGtesting.com
Printed in the USA
BVHW011915280821
615310BV00019B/337